Can You See the Beetle?

Matt Reher   Katie Axt

This is a beetle.

And this is a beetle.

There are lots of beetles.

Beetles look like where they live.

Beetles can live in the woods.

This beetle looks like a tree.

7

This beetle looks like the leaves.

Can you see the beetle?

Beetles can live at the beach.

This beetle looks like the sand.

This beetle looks like a rock.

Can you see the beetle?

Beetles can live in the grass.

This beetle looks like the grass.

This beetle looks like the flower.

Can you see the beetle?

snake

lizard

skunk

bird

bat

Lots of animals eat beetles.

Animals can't eat what they can't see.

Can you see the beetle?

Beetle Facts

Cucumber Beetles are yellow with black spots. They are often found on bean, squash, pumpkin, and cucumber plants. They blend into flowers such as sunflowers.

Tortoise Beetles have a flattened shell-like body that resembles a tortoise. They can be many colors and often blend in with leaves and flowers.

Weevils are beetles that have a long head forming a snout. Some have shiny hairs covering their bodies. Most weevils are brown or green, which helps them blend into the forest.

Ladybugs are small beetles found in gardens. They come in many different colors. Farmers love ladybugs because they eat plant-eating bugs.

Woodworm Beetles are often found on trees eating tree bark. They blend in because of their brown speckled coloring.

Hide Beetles look like rocks. They have short antennae and a hard shell which is black or brown. They can blend in with trees, rocks, and dirt.

Japanese Beetles have a hard metallic green shell and copper wings. They eat more than 300 species of plants, even poison ivy. Most Japanese beetles eat in groups and can destroy crops.

Matching Colors

yellow

green

brown

red